## ABOUT THE GULF AND ATLANTIC COASTS

Beaches are borders, inflection points, separations between enormous water bodies and our coastal landscapes. They also provide critical habitat to some of our most iconic native species, including Brown Pelicans, Ghost Crabs, Horseshoe Crabs, and so much more. This guide is intended as an introduction to the more-common plants and animals you'll encounter in our region.

## HOW OUR BEACHES FORMED

To create a beach you need two main things: water currents and available beach-making materials, such as crushed rock, shells, or fossils. Put simply, a beach forms when sand is deposited on barrier islands by ocean currents and pounding waves. Eventually, plant roots help hold down the material, and over time, wind sculpts the sand into dunes, which protect inland areas from storm surges.

## THREATS TO OUR BEACHES

Our beaches may be thousands of years old, but they are some of North America's most vulnerable ecosystems. Rising sea levels, development, and stronger storms threaten beaches along both the Atlantic Ocean and Gulf of Mexico. The more you know about the species listed in this guide, the more you can help them be more resilient in the face of future changes. To learn how to minimize your impact on our beach ecosystems, see the Beach Etiquette panel at the end of this guide.

## ORGANIZATIONS THAT PROTECT BEACHES

U.S. Fish and Wildlife Service (fws.gov)

National Audubon Society (audubon.org)

Florida Shorebird Alliance (flshorebirdalliance.org)

The Nature Conservancy (nature.org)

National Wildlife Federation (nwf.org)

T0123830

## ANATOMY OF A BEACH

### TIDES

Tides are essentially long, large waves driven by the gravitational pull of the moon. Because tides can have a major impact on how much of the beach is exposed during your visit, it's always a good idea to check the tide chart before any outing. Once you find a tide table online or at a local shop in your area, look up the date you plan to head to the beach and the high and low tide times.

### SUPRATIDAL ZONE

This part of the beach may be splashed by waves during high tide, but is almost never completely underwater.

### DRIFT LINE OR WRACK LINE

The area or "line" where shells or seagrass are left on the beach during high tide.

### INTERTIDAL ZONE

This section of the beach is underwater during high tide, but exposed during low tide. It is often divided into three zones: Upper, Middle, and Lower.

### SWASH/SURF ZONE

The area of the beach where the waves crash into the sand.

### SUBTIDAL ZONE

This zone is always covered by salt water.

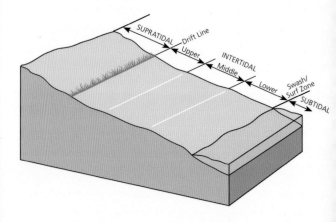

# BIRDS

Beaches host year-round avian residents, including everything from summer breeders and migratory visitors to winter species. In fact, you can identify the season by identifying which birds flock to the beaches!

To find beach birds, look for their silhouettes along three different planes: in the sky, soaring overhead; running along or standing on the beach itself; or floating on the waves off-shore. Different species utilize different areas as they rest, search for food, and raise their young.

Birds are best seen through binoculars or in a camera lens. Avoid spooking or scaring the birds—if they flush (fly away), the birds expend critical energy they need for finding food, and this can leave chicks or eggs vulnerable to the heat or predators. Give the birds their space, and do not feed them.

These are not all the possible birds you can spot on our beaches, but this is a good sampling of more-common species.

## GULLS

**Herring Gull**

**Laughing Gull**

**Ring-billed Gull**

**Bonaparte's Gull**
Non-breeding plumage

**Great Black-backed Gull★**
*Atlantic Coast

RAPTORS

**Osprey**

**Bald Eagle**

TERNS

**Least Tern**

**Royal Tern**

**Sandwich Tern**

**Caspian Tern**

**Common Tern**

**Forster's Tern**
Non-breeding plumage

**OTHER SEABIRDS**

**Brown Pelican**

**American White Pelican**

**Common Loon**
Non-breeding plumage

**Horned Grebe**
Non-breeding plumage

**Red-breasted Merganser**

**Double-crested Cormorant**

### WADING BIRDS

**Great Blue Heron**

**Great Egret**

**Snowy Egret**

**Reddish Egret**

**Little Blue Heron**

**Tricolored Heron**

### SHOREBIRDS

**Sanderling**

**Willet**

**Ruddy Turnstone**

**Snowy Plover**

**Wilson's Plover**

**American Oystercatcher**

## WHAT TO DO IF YOU SEE A BANDED BIRD

Scientists band birds to learn more about their life history and movement patterns. Each band is unique, and studying individuals allows researchers to track them over time. But that's only true if people submit their bird band observations!

Snowy Plover with bands on its legs

If you see a banded bird, photograph the bird's legs, or take notes on the colors of the bands, where they are on each leg, and any numbers and letters you see. Banded birds can be reported at www.reportband.gov

## SHELLS

There are hundreds of different kinds of shells that wash up on our beaches, but some are more common than others. Before you head out to the beach, check the local rules to make sure collecting is allowed. And wherever you are, remember: if there is a living creature within the shell, carefully place it back in the water.

The best time of year for shelling is in the spring and during low tide. However, shelling is also excellent after major storms have moved shells from farther offshore up onto the beaches, which can occur from late spring all the way until the end of November.

**Sand Dollar**

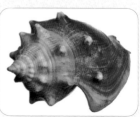

**Conch Shells**

**Junonia Shells**

**Lightning Whelk Shells**

**Cockle Shells**

**Tulip-banded Shells**

**Turkey Wing Shells**

**Murex Shells**

**Coquina Shells**

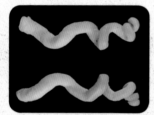

**Cerith Shells**

**Worm Snail Shells**

**Atlantic Slipper Shells**

**Limpets**

**Jingle Shells**

Calico Scallop

Florida Spiny Jewelbox

Oyster Shells

Marsh Periwinkle

Southern Quahog

Augers

Whelk Egg Case

Sea Bean

**Atlantic Jackknife Clam★**

*Atlantic Coast

**Sea Urchin**

**Coral Pieces**

## SEAGLASS

Beachcombing is a popular activity because you can find little pieces of history hidden within the sand: seaglass! Seaglass forms when wave action and sand smooth the sharp edges of glass fragments that were discarded in the ocean. This makes them safe to handle as well as beautiful. Brown, green, and white are the most common seaglass colors, while blue, red, and purple are harder to come by. Orange is the rarest seaglass hue.

Florida has more seaglass than any other state. Florida's Hutchinson Island is well known for its seaglass!

**Seaglass**

**Seaglass**

## SAND

Sand is formed from ground-up rocks, shells, and fossils, giving different beaches a unique look and feel.

### Quartz Sand

Often called "sugar sand," this sand originates from quartz, which gives it a bright-white color.

### Black (fossil)

The black patches of sand are formed by ground-up fossils.

### Coquina (orange)

Why is some sand orange? This hue—for which Daytona Beach is known—comes from the ground-up coquina shells that make up a large portion of this sand. The rusty color comes from iron oxide.

### Coral/Mussel

Beaches in the Keys and in Southeastern Florida have more coral and mussel pieces than quartz, which changes the feel of the sand.

## JELLYFISH

Don't touch! They may be beautiful, but avoid touching jellyfish whenever possible. Some species have very long tentacles that can be nearly invisible (especially in sand), so give jellyfish lots of space to avoid a sting.

Amazingly, only 5 percent of a jellyfish is actual body mass. Despite their pesky stings, jellyfish are critical food sources for sea turtles!

**Moon Jellyfish**

**Cannonball Jellyfish**

**Portuguese Man-of-war**

**Sea Nettle Jellyfish**

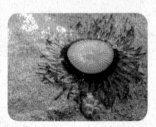

**Blue Button Jellyfish**

**By-the-wind Sailor Jellyfish**

**Mushroom Cap Jellyfish**

**Mauve Stinger**

**Box Jellyfish**

## SEAHORSES

**Lined Seahorse**

**Dwarf Seahorse**

**Longsnout Seahorse**

## CRABS

Look along most expanses of beach and you'll likely be able to spot crabs. From the Ghost Crabs that skitter along the beach to the Sand Fleas buried in the sand, crabs are a common sight along our beaches.

**Ghost Crab**

**Blue Crab**

**Sand Fleas**

**Gulf Stone Crab**

**Atlantic Rock Crab★**
*Atlantic Coast

**Horseshoe Crab★**
*Atlantic Coast. While they look like crabs, they are more closely related to spiders.

## SHARKS

There are many sharks in our waters, but negative interactions with sharks are incredibly rare. In fact, they play an important role in nearshore, offshore, and reef ecosystems, acting as the apex predator. To stay extra safe, swim where there are lifeguards present, exit the water if a shark has been spotted, and don't harass a shark in any way.

Looking to find shark teeth? Venice Beach, FL, is known for its shark teeth, as are the beaches around Jacksonville, Topsail Beach in North Carolina, and Folly Beach in South Carolina.

**Great Hammerhead Shark**

**Tiger Shark**

**Scalloped Hammerhead**

**Bull Shark**

**Great White Shark**

**Lemon Shark**

**Sandbar Shark**

**Reef Shark★**
*Florida Keys

**Black Tip Shark**

**Dusky Shark**

## FISH

Fishing is a popular activity on many of our beaches, whether you're shore fishing, booking a charter, or fishing from a designated pier. Before casting a line, ensure you have a license and are familiar with the local fishing regulations/bag limits.

**Pompano**

**Redfish**

**Tarpon**

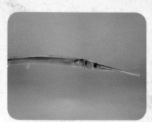

**Needlefish**

**Mullet**

**Spanish Mackerel**

**Ladyfish**

**Spotted Sea Trout**

**Sheepshead**

**Southern Flounder**

**Gulf Kingfish**

**Bluefish**

**Black Drum**

**Gafftopsail Catfish★**

*use caution when handling; it has venomous barbs

**Croaker**

**Pinfish**

**False Albacore**

**Crevalle Jack**

## SEA TURTLES AND OTHER ICONIC ANIMALS

Sea turtles swim offshore as they feed, and during the summer months, females haul themselves onto the beach during the night to dig holes with powerful flippers before depositing golf-ball size eggs. The baby turtles hatch during the night as well, using light reflected off the waves to guide them back to the sea. If you see an adult, baby turtle, or egg—don't touch it! Interfering with them in any way is illegal.

Do you live along the beach? Both adult and baby sea turtles can mistake house lights for the moon and stars, causing them to move in the wrong direction. Turn out your lights at night, or replace them with amber-colored bulbs, to help sea turtles in your area have a successful nesting season.

**Loggerhead Sea Turtle**

**Green Sea Turtle**

**Leatherback Sea Turtle**

**Hawksbill Sea Turtle**

**Kemp's Ridley Sea Turtle**

This turtle is pictured with a tracking device. That helps scientists learn more about this rare creature!

*All of these turtles are protected under the Endangered Species Act.

## MANATEES

**Manatee**

Manatees are mammals that can be spotted along the Gulf of Mexico or Atlantic Ocean when they are on the move between seasons. Though they are large, they are very gentle, eating only grasses and vegetation.

## ALLIGATORS

**American Alligator**

Wait, alligators can swim in the ocean? Yes! Though it is less common, American Alligators can use water routes near beaches and bays to move from one fresh-water habitat to another.

## DOLPHINS

**Bottlenose Dolphin**

Common Bottlenose Dolphins often feed in the waves near shore, and can be spotted as they surface to breathe or when they jump into the air. *Note:* if you're looking for whales, they are not often spotted in our region. Your best bet is in the winter along the Atlantic Coast.

## RAYS

**Rays**

Rays and skates are commonly seen in the shallows, flying through the water. Don't touch, however, as some rays (stingrays) have venomous barbs.

## PLANTS

Plants play critical roles on our beaches and in nearshore ecosystems. Their roots hold sand in place, allowing for the creation of dunes. Seaweed not only creates habitat, it also provides a critical food and shelter source for beach organisms when it washes up onto the beach. If you see these plants on the beach, admire them from a safe distance, don't pick them, and avoid disturbing dune areas.

**Railroad Vine**

**Sea Oats**

**Smooth Cordgrass**

**Sargassum Seaweed**

**Rushes**

**Common Reed**

## BUTTERFLIES

Did you know that we can see butterflies on our beaches? While not always present, some species migrate across the open water, while others are attracted to the flowering plants that grow within the dunes or on the coastline.

### Monarch

One of the most famous butterflies in the country, this species is known to migrate long distances. Florida also hosts a year-round population.

### Gulf Fritillary

Orange on top, with beautiful white spots underneath, this is a common butterfly in Florida.

### Long-tailed Skipper

This butterfly migrates up the Atlantic Coast and into the Southeast in summer, then retreats into Florida for the winter months.

### Common Buckeye

Buckeyes love a very open, very sunny habitat–like dunes and coastal areas with low-lying vegetation.

## BEACH SAFETY

Before you head out, check out the surf and weather conditions (including UV levels). Pay special attention to the flag systems on public beaches. A double red-flag means the beach is closed. A red flag notes a high hazard due to strong currents or high surf. A yellow flag indicates a medium hazard (moderate conditions). A green flag is displayed when conditions are calm. A purple flag informs visitors that jellyfish or other stinging creatures are present. When in doubt, ask lifeguards or other authorities for clarification.

## RIP CURRENTS

Rip currents, sometimes called "rip tides," are a perennial concern, especially after storms. Put simply, a rip current is an area of current that moves away from the beach and into the ocean. Rip currents are essentially narrow channels of fast-moving water that can overtake even the best swimmers, dragging them into the open ocean. They often occur near structures, such as piers or jetties, so don't swim near them.

If you're caught in a rip tide, don't panic. Instead, signal/yell for assistance, and swim **parallel** to the shore, not directly against the current. (Fighting a rip current would simply tire you out.) Rip currents are rarely more than 80 feet wide, so once you're free of the current, you should be able to turn and swim toward shore.

If you suspect someone's in trouble in the water, immediately notify a lifeguard and/or call 9-1-1.

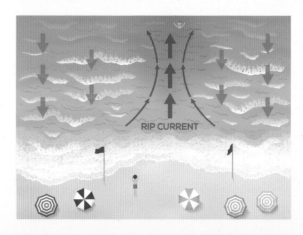

RIP CURRENT

## TRASH

Our beaches are a treasure, so please do your best to take care of them. When you're at the beach, have a leave-no-trace ethic and be sure to pack out all of your trash and recyclables. Marine trash can maim or even kill wildlife.

## DON'T HARASS WILDLIFE

We share beaches with a variety of wildlife; whenever possible, simply admire beach life from a distance. This ensures our beaches will stay healthy for years to come.

## DOGS

Dogs can be allowed on beaches, but many have restrictions to protect wildlife. Before you bring your pup, check ahead of time if dogs are allowed, and once you're at the beach, keep your dog on a leash and clean up after your pet. During nesting season, it is especially important to keep dogs away from birds, as they can damage nests, injure chicks, and frighten parents away.

## BIRDS

Birdwatching is a delight on beaches, but give them their space. Watch birds from a considerate distance using binoculars or a camera. When children or dogs run after birds and cause them to fly (this is known as flushing), it causes them to use valuable energy. Additionally, during nesting season, flushed adult birds often leave behind nests, eggs, and chicks, which are vulnerable to both heat and predators.

## ERIKA ZAMBELLO

From her home base in North Florida, Erika Zambello has explored hundreds of ecological research sites, estuarine research reserves, national parks, state parks, and national wildlife refuges across the Southeast and around the country. She was a National Geographic Young Explorer and serves on the board of the National Parks Traveler. She holds a Master's Degree in Environmental Management from the Duke Nicholas School of the Environment (where she specialized in Ecosystem Science and Conservation) and a Master's Degree in Strategic Communication from the University of West Florida. As a writer, her work has been featured in *National Geographic Adventure, National Geographic Voices, Backpacker, Florida Sportsman,* and more.

*Adventure Quick Guides*

# Discover Animals, Plants, Seashells, and More!

Organized by group for quick
and easy identification

## Simple and convenient—
## open the correct tab to identify your finds

- Pocket-size format—easier than laminated foldouts

- Professional photos of each object or species

- Easy-to-use information for even casual observers

- Expert author who specializes in ecosystem science

Get these *Adventure Quick Guides* for your area

NATURE / COASTAL LIFE / SOUTH

ISBN 978-1-64755-187-2    **$9.95 U.S.**

5 0 9 9 5

9 781647 551872

PUBLICATIONS
**Adventure**
an imprint of AdventureKEEN